My Menopause Moments

A 30-DAY COLLECTION OF MY THOUGHTS WHILE
NAVIGATING THROUGH THE EXTREMITIES OF
MENOPAUSE

I0456510

TRAVONDA DAVENPORT

www.TrueVinePublishing.org

My Menopause Moments
Travonda Davenport

Published by
True Vine Publishing
810 Dominican Dr
Nashville, TN 37228
www.TrueVinePublishing.org

ISBN: 978-1-962783-46-0 Paperback
ISBN: 978-1-962783-47-7 eBook

Printed in the United States of America—First Printing

Acknowledgment and Dedication

To all those who pick up this book, thank you for giving my words a chance and to every reader who finds a piece of themselves within these journals."

To my husband, who has walked every step of this journey with me.

To my family and friends for your support and encouragement.

To my Lord and Savior, Jesus Christ; WE DID IT!

To myself, for showing up, pushing through, and finishing what I started.

DAY 1

As I pick my clothes for the day,

Must I wear something light and thin?

I understand that it is winter,

But this battle I can't win.

You dictate my mood.

I'm happy and then suddenly sad.

I cry about everything,

Even the straight teeth I never had.

So I will pick my clothes,

Light and thin it has to be.

As for the rest of the week,

We just have to wait and see.

MENOPAUSE REFLECTION

Does menopause dictate what you wear for the day or to a certain event? If so, how has this made you feel?

_____

_____

_____

_____

_____

_____

_____

_____

_____

_____

_____

_____

_____

_____

_____

_____

_____

_____

_____

_____

_____

_____

DAY 2

"Hormonal Imbalance,"

What the hell does that mean?

Why must I endure this experience?

Shouldn't there be a vaccine?

"Hormonal Imbalance,"

Why can't my body just push reject?

It has invaded my space.

I want to kick out this intruder,

But its origin, I cannot trace.

"Hormonal Imbalance"

please just let me be.

I never extended you the invitation

to share my body with me.

MENOPAUSE REFLECTION

DID YOU KNOW...

Menopause is a stage in a woman's life where, due to decreased estrogen levels, she stops ovulating, having a period, and she is no longer fertile. This phase is notorious for causing hormonal shifts and imbalances that result in frustrating side effects such as hot flashes, mood swings, and decreased libido.

_____

_____

_____

_____

_____

_____

_____

_____

_____

_____

_____

_____

_____

_____

_____

_____

_____

DAY 3

My libido is gone.

Can't find it anywhere.

I'm dry as the desert,

Does anyone even care?

My libido is gone.

Oh where could it be?

I've looked all over.

I think it's hiding from me.

My libido is gone.

How do I contact the news?

Missing libido report.

I don't want to accuse.

Reward will be given.

Let's act real fast.

My libido is gone.

Without it, I can't last.

MENOPAUSE REFLECTION

How has low libido affected intimacy in your relationship? Has it affected how you feel about yourself as a woman?

_____

_____

_____

_____

_____

_____

_____

_____

_____

_____

_____

_____

_____

_____

_____

_____

_____

_____

DAY 4

My fan is my best friend.

It provides comfort day and night.

When I'm awakened by hot flashes,

It makes me feel alright.

My fan is my best friend.

It never lets me down.

It has different cooling speeds

And a very soothing sound.

My fan is my best friend.

I need it everyday.

I never felt this way before.

Please never go away.

My fan is my best friend.

It only seeks to please.

Off and on it goes

It understands my needs.

MENOPAUSE REFLECTION

DID YOU KNOW...

Sleeplessness due to menopause is often associated with hot flashes. These sensations of extreme heat can come on during the day or at night. Nighttime hot flashes are often paired with unexpected awakenings.

_____

_____

_____

_____

_____

_____

_____

_____

_____

_____

_____

_____

_____

_____

_____

_____

_____

_____

_____

DAY 5

I wake up itching
From head to toe.
I scratch here and I scratch there,
But it never wants to go
Away and give me peace.
What's a girl to do?
Keep your nails groomed and ready
Because you have no clue.
It will strike again;
Itching with no relief.
Who would have thought menopause
Could cause such grief?
I scratch here and I scratch there,
And find no peace anywhere.

MENOPAUSE REFLECTION

DID YOU KNOW...

During menopause, a drop in estrogen levels can cause your body to produce less collagen and natural oils. This, in turn, can cause your skin to become itchy.

_____

_____

_____

_____

_____

_____

_____

_____

_____

_____

_____

_____

_____

_____

_____

_____

_____

_____

_____

DAY 6

My ceiling has become a canvas.

What will I paint tonight?

Random thoughts fill my mind,

Wondering if things will turn out right.

Who needs sleep?

Something so precious and rare;

It has abandoned me

Since menopause doesn't care.

Melatonin doesn't work for me.

It's nothing more than free candy.

I will just hold on tight.

My ceiling has become a canvas.

What will I paint tonight?

MENOPAUSE REFLECTION

If you could paint a picture to express your feelings about menopause, what would it look like?

_____

_____

_____

_____

_____

_____

_____

_____

_____

_____

_____

_____

_____

_____

_____

_____

_____

_____

_____

_____

DAY 7

Today is a good day.

I was able to sleep all night.

I woke up dry and refreshed,

Feeling that everything will be alright.

Today is a good day,

Emotions all intact.

I did my devotion,

Drank my coffee,

God's got my back.

Today is a good day.

At least that's what I thought.

As I was preparing for a zoom meeting,

I started feeling hot.

It started in my feet and quickly ran up my legs.

Before I could grab the fan,

Heat was all on my head.

Today was a good day.

Or so I thought.

MENOPAUSE REFLECTION

Have you started your day off on a positive note and then somehow it went left? How did you handle it and were you able to get things back on track?

_____

_____

_____

_____

_____

_____

_____

_____

_____

_____

_____

_____

_____

_____

_____

_____

_____

_____

_____

_____

_____

DAY 8

My husband has a different wife.
He doesn't know what to do.
I don't have the words to explain to him
What I'm actually going through.
He touches me and I draw back
I'm certainly not in the mood.
Menopause has taken a toll.
Don't judge me and be shrewd.
I'm praying that he stays
For better or for worse.
I remind him everyday,
This seems like some curse.
I'm off and then I'm on.
He's tired of the ride,
But what am I to do?
No control of the hormones inside.
My husband has a different wife.
I'm not sure who she is.
We both need to confront her together.
And remind her I am his.
Menopause is her name.
I'm sure its written in the hall of fame.

MENOPAUSE REFLECTION

Has menopause created issues with you and your spouse? If so, how do you handle it? If not, how would you rate the intimate connection with your spouse while dealing with menopause?

_____

_____

_____

_____

_____

_____

_____

_____

_____

_____

_____

_____

_____

_____

_____

_____

_____

_____

_____

DAY 9

Menopause anxiety,

They give everything a name,

But when I tell you,

Nothing has been the same.

Anxiety crept in like a thief

And had caused me so much grief.

I shake and sweat at the same time,

But I'm a confident woman

Working and hustling for mine.

This will not control or dictate my mood.

You are being extremely rude,

But I got you,

And I understand your cause.

Just give me a minute to pause

And devise a plan.

Your eviction papers

Are definitely in hand.

MENOPAUSE REFLECTION

DID YOU KNOW...

Anxiety is a common symptom of menopause. Hormone changes, life stresses, and sleep problems may all cause anxiety during this time.

_____

_____

_____

_____

_____

_____

_____

_____

_____

_____

_____

_____

_____

_____

_____

_____

_____

_____

_____

_____

DAY 10

I can't remember a thing,

And I'm tired of writing a list:

To do, to do, to do,

Without it, I'm taking a risk.

Cause I can't remember a thing.

Where did I leave my keys?

Are they in my purse?

Can someone help me please?

I can't remember a thing.

Appointment and things to do at work.

I need a magic pill

Menopause is a jerk.

I can't remember a thing.

It's like a blank space in my brain.

Plug me in for an immediate download

Before I go insane.

I can't remember a thing.

MENOPAUSE REFLECTION

DID YOU KNOW...

Brain fog, or cognitive impairment, is a common symptom of menopause that can affect up to two-thirds of women. It can include problems with: concentration, decision-making, learning and retaining information, thinking clearly, forgetfulness, misplacing items, and time lapses.

_____

_____

_____

_____

_____

_____

_____

_____

_____

_____

_____

_____

_____

_____

_____

_____

_____

_____

DAY 11

Ready, Set, NO!

I'm dressed and ready to go:

Hair done and makeup too,

Jewelry matching and I'm wearing blue.

I'm dressed and ready to go,

Got on my comfortable shoes,

Did my daily affirmation,

I'm a winner and won't lose.

I'm dressed and ready to go.

Then, a hot flash hit me.

I'm sweating, my clothes are sticking.

I won't be going far.

I was dressed and ready to go,

But menopause said

Ready, Set, NO!

MENOPAUSE REFLECTION

Menopause had the power to shift my day at any moment and that bothered me. How are you handling the unpredictable surprises that menopause brings?

_____

_____

_____

_____

_____

_____

_____

_____

_____

_____

_____

_____

_____

_____

_____

_____

_____

_____

Day 12

I was excited to have no period;

No tampons anymore.

I was excited to have no period,

And throw my monthly apps out the door.

I was excited to have no period;

No more cramps and feeling bad.

I was excited to have no period.

This was the best feeling I ever had,

But much to my surprise,

My period was replaced

Without my permission.

Menopause invaded my space.

I was excited to have no period

But now I want it back.

Bring the cramps, tampons, bloating

And all the midnight snacks.

Can I do a reversal or go back in time?

I was excited to have no period,

But I was really out of my mind!

MENOPAUSE REFLECTION

What do you miss about not having your period that you would trade with a menopause symptom?

_____

_____

_____

_____

_____

_____

_____

_____

_____

_____

_____

_____

_____

_____

_____

_____

_____

_____

_____

DAY 13

Ready, Set, NO!

You better hold on tight.

I just hit my 50's,

This doesn't seem quite right.

Ready, Set, NO!

Gravity has taken a toll.

Push them up,

Tuck it in,

I can not hide my rolls.

Ready, Set, NO!

Deodorant must be strong;

Extra perfume and body wash

Does not last all day long.

Ready, Set, NO!

Hair now on my face and neck.

It's falling out everywhere else.

What the heck?

Ready, Set, NO!

I might as well submit

Needless to say most days I feel like S***!

MENOPAUSE REFLECTION

DID YOU KNOW...

Specifically, the declining estrogen levels during menopause can significantly affect hair growth. This includes thinning hair on the scalp and increased growth of unwanted facial hair, such as "peach fuzz" and dark, coarse hair often appearing on the upper lip and chin. The hair on their scalp thins, while the chin or upper lip sprouts patches of "peach fuzz" to extremely coarse hair. In fact, the results of one study show that nearly 40% of women aged 45 years and older experience unwanted facial hair growth.

DAY 14

I am one with my body.

I am her.

We are we.

I am one with my body.

In every way He created me to be.

I am one with my body,

Today and forevermore.

We are going through a transition,

But we won't hit the floor.

Menopause has driven us apart

And invaded our space.

This is temporary.

We will win this race.

I'm one with my body.

I am her.

We are we.

I'm one with my body.

I'm making this decree.

MENOPAUSE REFLECTION

What does it mean for you to be one with your body? Has this been difficult since menopause? If so, how?

_____

_____

_____

_____

_____

_____

_____

_____

_____

_____

_____

_____

_____

_____

_____

_____

_____

_____

_____

_____

_____

DAY 15

My skin is brown,
With blemishes here and there,
My skin is oily,
With strings of hair.
Growing out of my chin and now on my neck;
Is this really what menopause does?
What the heck?
My skin is brown
With blemishes here and there.
Cleanser, moisturizer and serum
Seem to get me nowhere.
Make up shades from light to dark
Concealer and primer
All play their part
In my daily routine,
And I can't skip a step.
I need to feel pretty
Because menopause doesn't help.
My skin is brown,
And I love it all.
Menopause can't touch that.
I'm still standing tall.

MENOPAUSE REFLECTION

DID YOU KNOW...

Menopause, which officially begins one year after your last period, can bring with it some noticeable changes to your skin and hair. As hormone levels plummet, your skin can become dry, slack, and thin. You may notice more hair on your face and less on your scalp. With the right care, you can lessen these effects.

_____

_____

_____

_____

_____

_____

_____

_____

_____

_____

_____

_____

_____

_____

_____

_____

_____

_____

DAY 16

My va-jay-jay has no voice.

She has submitted to the stronger.

Menopause has taken over.

It doesn't have much longer.

We are devising a plan,

My va-jay-jay and I.

We're taking menopause down

After this one last cry.

My va-jay-jay has no voice.

She cries everyday.

I hear her in my sleep.

She wants to get away

From the pressure and the

Worries that menopause brings.

I told her to hold on,

It won't be long before we sing,

How we made it over.

Back in the game again

We will make it through this

And together we win.

MENOPAUSE REFLECTION

If your va-jay-jaya could talk to you about menopause, what would she say or what song would she sing?

_____

_____

_____

_____

_____

_____

_____

_____

_____

_____

_____

_____

_____

_____

_____

_____

_____

_____

_____

_____

_____

_____

DAY 17

I keep gaining weight

In front but not the back.

I never seem to gain

In the places where I lack.

I keep gaining weight.

Elastic is my friend.

Eating chocolate chip cookies in bed

Seems to have no end.

I keep gaining weight.

The numbers don't lie.

Up and up they go.

Don't you dare ask me why.

No I'm not pregnant,

And I'm not on any meds.

Menopause has me in a head lock,

And it's just like I said.

I keep gaining weight

In the front but not the back.

I never seem to gain

In the places where I lack.

MENOPAUSE REFLECTION

DID YOU KNOW...

The hormonal changes of menopause tend to make it more likely that women will gain weight around the abdomen, rather than the hips and thighs.

DAY 18

What's going on with all this aching?

I wake up and can barely move.

My bones ache so bad,

I have to finally choose

To move despite the pain,

And start my day with praise.

Just to be alive is a great blessing

In these crazy days.

Menopause has no mercy,

Nor does it discriminate.

It deals with all of us differently,

Regardless of color or age.

So I exercise everyday

In order to win this fight

I refuse to give in to menopause.

It just doesn't seem right.

The aches have somehow lessened,

And I've made it another day.

Menopause is unruly

And seems to be here to stay.

MENOPAUSE REFLECTIONS

What are some physical symptoms that you have as a result of menopause? How have you handled it?

_____

_____

_____

_____

_____

_____

_____

_____

_____

_____

_____

_____

_____

_____

_____

_____

_____

_____

_____

_____

_____

_____

_____

DAY 19

Hot, cold, hot, cold

Covers on and covers off.

I'm sweating and then I'm freezing,

Which usually ends with a cough.

My body can't adjust

To this new normal place,

So I scheduled a meeting with menopause,

But realized it had no face.

I checked my ring camera,

And it wasn't there.

I was willing to meet virtually,

But it really didn't care.

It invaded my body anyway,

Then threatened me with a dare.

I scheduled a meeting with menopause,

And she was a no show.

Sent me a text message

That she was waiting but had to go.

Hot, cold, hot, cold

Is this what happens when you get old?

MENOPAUSE REFLECTION

DID YOU KNOW....

Changing hormone levels during perimenopause and menopause likely cause your hypothalamus (the part of the brain that controls your body heat) to have trouble regulating your body temperature. Think of it as a glitch in your body's internal thermostat. You may feel sudden warmth or a flush in your face, neck and chest. In response, your body tries to cool itself by sweating too much.

_____

_____

_____

_____

_____

_____

_____

_____

_____

_____

_____

_____

_____

_____

_____

DAY 20

Tiredness and fatigue;
The gifts that keep on giving.
How in the world am I supposed to keep living
This life with no energy or desire do a thing?
They say it's not depression,
but only if I could sing.
The song would be "Good Morning Gorgeous"
I'm ready to do my thing.
If I could finally get a break,
But this menopause, I can't shake.
No completion or end date.
just let it have its way.
It's unruly and has no mercy,
As if it wants to stay around
and be your new BFF.
Does your opinion really matter?
Menopause ignores you,
and all of the chatter.
Tiredness and fatigue;
The gifts that keep on giving.
I'm glad that I'm still
In the land of the living.

MENOPAUSE REFLECTION

DID YOU KNOW...

Fatigue is a common symptom of menopause, affecting 85.3% of women in one study. It can be physical, mental, or both, and can feel like constant exhaustion or burnout.

_____

_____

_____

_____

_____

_____

_____

_____

_____

_____

_____

_____

_____

_____

_____

_____

_____

_____

DAY 21

Supplements and pills;
Nothing seems to work.
It's all just a temporary fix
With a small perk.
I'm ready to feel normal
And not all over the place.
Doing my own well check call,
God give me the grace
To make it another day.
With this, I have no control.
Some days I feel like I'm
Being pulled in a hole.
God has my back,
And I can see the break of day.
With him by my side,
I know there's a way
To keep things moving,
And trust it will be ok.
Supplements and pills,
I take them every night,
Praying my hormones will respond.
I hopeful that things will work out right.

MENOPAUSE REFLECTION

Do you take any supplements or hormone replacement pills? How have they made you feel?

_____

_____

_____

_____

_____

_____

_____

_____

_____

_____

_____

_____

_____

_____

_____

_____

_____

_____

_____

_____

_____

DAY 22

If my va-jay-jay had a voice,
It would have no choice
But to tell the whole truth.
How I wish we could go back to our youth.
Things were simple, and the flow was free,
But now I'm discombobulated.
What the hell is wrong with me?
If my va-jay-jay had a voice,
It would have no choice
But to tell the truth
And connect to a Bluetooth
So that everyone can hear,
From far away and those near.
The uncertainty is real—
Menopause has come to steal
Your joy and peace of mind.
Just hang on,
Because in due time,
You will win this fight.
But for now,
Peace, love, and to all of us,
A cool night.

MENOPAUSE REFLECTION

If your va-jay-jay had a voice, what concern would domi-
nate the conversation?

_____

_____

_____

_____

_____

_____

_____

_____

_____

_____

_____

_____

_____

_____

_____

_____

_____

_____

_____

_____

DAY 23

Hot flashes and night sweats

Go hand in hand.

Why do women have to deal with this?

Does God really understand?

I have a serious attitude,

And I don't want to talk.

Just give me some space—

Maybe I'll go for a walk.

Hot flashes and night sweats

Go hand in hand.

I will never embrace this

While I'm in the land

Of the living.

I will fight them both

And take them down.

When I'm done,

They will no longer be around.

Hot flashes and night sweats.

MENOPAUSE REFLECTION

Hot flashes and night sweats have made it very uncomfortable for me to do anything, especially sleep. In what ways has it been uncomfortable for you? Do you experience both hot flashes and night sweats?

_____

DAY 24

Menopause stage indicator—
What the hell will they think of next?
You pee on a stick
As if you're pregnant.
I'm sure you can guess the rest:
Pre, early, late, or post-menopause,
The stick will let you know.
I feel like I'm all of them.
Ready, set—the answer is no.
Menopause stage indicator,
As if knowing really helps a thing.
You still have to go through the process,
So you might as well sing
"I'm Not Gon' Cry" by Mary J.,
Get some ice cream,
And another workday.
It's like playing Ms. Pac-Man.
You have to know which way to go.
When it comes for you,
Go left, go right,
Eat the blinking light.
Then your strength will come,
The battle will be won,
And those things will be alright.

MENOPAUSE REFLECTION

DID YOU KNOW...

Over the 10-day span, the Menopause Stage Indicator test monitors a woman's changing levels of FSH and, based on general hormone levels calibrated by age, informs her about which stage of menopause she might be in: premenopause, early perimenopause, late perimenopause, or postmenopause

_____

_____

_____

_____

_____

_____

_____

_____

_____

_____

_____

_____

_____

_____

_____

_____

_____

_____

DAY 25

I'm super sensitive

About stupid, crazy things.

I want what I want—

Garlic parmesan chicken wings.

I don't care about the weight.

I just want to snack.

It's really uncontrollable.

I actually feel attacked

By menopause,

Like I'm in a chokehold,

Waiting for me to give in

And grow really old.

But I'm eating my spinach

Like Popeye the Sailor Man.

I am what I am,

And that's all that I am.

I'm super sensitive about stupid, crazy things.

Don't come for me

Without garlic parmesan chicken wings.

MENOPAUSE REFLECTION

Have you had pregnancy-like cravings while dealing with menopause? If so, what are they?

_____

_____

_____

_____

_____

_____

_____

_____

_____

_____

_____

_____

_____

_____

_____

_____

_____

_____

_____

_____

_____

DAY 26

I struggle wanting to go to bed.

It's hard to get to sleep

With my satin bonnet on my head.

This is really deep.

The heat begins to travel,

And it doesn't miss a spot.

Cover on, cover off—

I'm still trying to connect the dots.

This is the game that we play.

Most nights it lasts

Till the break of day.

Sleep is something strange

That I know no more.

I'm good to get 3 hours in

Before my feet hit the floor.

I just keep it moving.

Less sleep has become my thing.

It gives me more time to eat

Another extra chicken wing.

MENOPAUSE REFLECTION

DID YOU KNOW...

If you are over the age of 40 and have trouble sleeping, wake up hot and sweaty, or feel tired during the day, you are not alone. Menopause—the time in life when a person's periods stop for 12 consecutive months—brings about a series of changes, including shifts in sleep patterns.

As many as 46% of individuals experience sleep difficulties in the years leading up to menopause. Following menopause, about half of people report sleep disorders. Understanding the intersection of menopause and sleep is crucial for those navigating this transformative period.

DAY 27

I'm wet,

I'm dry.

I want to laugh,

I want to cry.

I'm fat,

I'm thin.

This battle

I can't win.

I'm in,

I'm out.

What is this really about?

I'm hot,

I'm cold.

Is this what happens

When we get old?

MENOPAUSE REFLECTION

If you could assess how you are feeling at this very moment, after reading this what would you say?

_____

_____

_____

_____

_____

_____

_____

_____

_____

_____

_____

_____

_____

_____

_____

_____

_____

_____

_____

_____

_____

DAY 28

I'm 52 with a long life ahead.

I'm a committed wife and mother.

With that being said,

There has been a disruption

To my life overall.

Sometimes I feel like I want to crawl

In a hole and never come out,

Or just scream and shout.

God, I need you every day,

Especially when menopause

Gets in the way.

Things will get better—

This won't last always.

I keep my head lifted

While wiping my tears,

Knowing that He is bigger

Than all my fears.

I'm 52 with a long life ahead.

MENOPAUSE REFLECTION

How do you keep your emotions in check while dealing with menopause, especially since it affects women emotionally?

_____

_____

_____

_____

_____

_____

_____

_____

_____

_____

_____

_____

_____

_____

_____

_____

_____

_____

_____

_____

_____

DAY 29

I get up to start my day

Read my devotion

And start to pray

Thanking God for making a way

Affirming and reminding myself

Of who he has created me to be

Menopause ignored the memo

And made it's own decree

As if we are one

Let's just wait and see

I have served an eviction notice

Signed sealed and delivered

To my most inner part

I had to break the relationship

It wasn't good for my heart.

MENOPAUSE REFLECTION

Take a moment and write menopause a short letter. This is a form of journaling and can be very therapeutic.

_____

_____

_____

_____

_____

_____

_____

_____

_____

_____

_____

_____

_____

_____

_____

_____

_____

_____

_____

_____

DAY 30

Melanin poppin',
Brows arched,
Lips shiny,
And makeup matte.
Where in this lineup
Do you see menopause at?
This should not be
A part
Of my daily routine.
Don't ask me what I mean.
If this was like makeup,
I would wash it off
And never
Use it again.
Instead, it's like
An unwelcome guest,
Laying around my house
And stealing all my rest.
Melanin poppin',
Brows arched,
Lips shiny,
And make up matte.
If you see menopause sneaking around,
Hit her with a bat.

MENOPAUSE REFLECTION

Hot flashes ruin all of my makeup, which frustrates my day. How has menopause frustrated you?

_____

_____

_____

_____

_____

_____

_____

_____

_____

_____

_____

_____

_____

_____

_____

_____

_____

_____

_____

_____

_____

_____

MENOPAUSE MOMENTS

DID YOU KNOW...
Resource Sites

DAY 2

Mira Fertility. (2019, December 10). *Hormonal imbalance signs, causes and treatments*. https://www.miracare.com/blog/hormone-imbalance/#:~:text=causes%20hormonal%20imbalance%3F-

DAY 4

Aliabadi, T. (2023, August 11). *Sleep disorders and menopause*. Dr. Aliabadi, Best Los Angeles OBGYN, Surgeon. https://www.draliabadi.com/menopause/menopausal-sleep-disorders/

DAY 5

Jay, K. (2023, May 5). Does menopause cause itchy skin? Plus, tips for managing itchiness. *Healthline*. https://www.healthline.com/health/menopause/menopause-itching#:~:text=Menopause%20and%20itching&text=Estrogen%20is%20related%20to%20the

DAY 9

Medical News Today. (2017, May 21). *Menopause and anxiety: What is the link?* https://www.medicalnewstoday.com/articles/317552#summary

DAY 10

UCLA Health. (2021, September 29). *Many women have cognition issues during menopause*. https://www.uclahealth.org/news/article/many-women-have-cognition-issues-during-menopause#:~:text=In%20fact%2C%20it

DAY 13

Perm Editor. (2023, February 2). Menopause and unwanted facial hair growth. *Permanence Hair Removal*. https://permanence.com.au/menopause-and-unwanted-facial-hair-causes-and-treatment-options/

DAY 15

American Academy of Dermatology. (n.d.). *Caring for your skin in menopause*. https://www.aad.org/public/everyday-care/skin-care-secrets/anti-aging/skin-care-during-menopause#:~:text=board%2Dcertified%20dermatologists.-

DAY 17

Better Health Victoria. (n.d.). *Menopause and weight gain*. https://www.betterhealth.vic.gov.au/health/conditionsandtreatments/menopause-and-weight-gain

DAY 19

Cleveland Clinic. (n.d.). *Night sweats: Menopause, other causes & treatment*. https://my.clevelandclinic.org/health/symptoms/16562-night-sweats

DAY 20

Medical News Today. (2021, October 7). *Menopause fatigue: Causes, treatment, and supplements*. https://www.medicalnewstoday.com/articles/menopause-fatigue

DAY 24

Time. (2023, August 31). *There's now an at-home menopause test, but is it necessary?* https://time.com/6310046/at-home-menopause-test/

DAY 26

Sleep Foundation. (2021, January 22). *How can menopause affect sleep?* https://www.sleepfoundation.org/women-sleep/menopause-and-sleep#:~:text=If%20you%20are%20over%20the